Strong Like a Pansy

Words by Oshri Liron Hakak
Art by Phyllis Karmas

BUTTERFLYON BOOKS

Strong Like a Pansy
Written by Oshri Liron Hakak,
Illustrated by Phyllis Karmas

Published by Butterflyon Books
Los Angeles
ISBN 978-1-964420-05-9

For pansies of all kinds.

You are strong!

Strong Like a Pansy

Be strong like the pansy you are...
how strong is the pansy you are!

A pansy's a flower
always bursting with color.

In the garden, in brightness,
they support one another.

I never did hear of a pansy who lied,

and their roots grow deeper
when they openly cry.

Be strong like the pansy you are…
how strong is the pansy you are!

Being tough, for a pansy,
means supporting the bees.

Power to the pansy
means sway with the breeze.

A pansy feels safe
wearing its heart on its sleeve,

takes time in the chaos
to love and to breathe.

Be strong like the pansy you are…
how strong is the pansy you are!

A pansy is humble
and causes no one to stumble,

forgives and gives back
when little bees bumble and fumble,

celebrates when its sister
or brother have won,

knows each take our turn
as the lucky one.

Be strong like the pansy you are…
how strong is the pansy you are!

A pansy doesn't mind
when its colors shine out,

nor does a pansy hide
an honest good pout.

A pansy sees strength
in delicate being,

and can grace a whole field
with its dance, so freeing.

Be strong like the pansy you are…
how strong is the pansy you are!

(FRI)END

Questions for Contemplation and Blooming

What does strength mean to you?

What qualities do you value most in others and yourself?

In what ways do you want to grow and develop?

How is kindness a kind of strength?

What is a great example of kindness in your life? (This could be a person who comes to mind, or a story about kindness.)

What are my favorite ways to be kind? What are my favorite ways to receive kindness?

How could things be different in the world if more people thought of kindness as a way to be strong?

Gratitude

Big thanks to Karim Shuquem for your support with making this book blossom into existence!

Here is a bit about Karim and Graphic Non-Violence:

Graphic Non-Violence provides socially engaged art education nationally, online and locally in Los Angeles. For Graphic Non-Violence, social engagement applies to the work we do with neurodivergent artists, as well as what we do to connect our students' art production with socially-minded projects such as this one. Thank you for being a part of our journey!

Visit us at   graphicnonviolence.com

About the Artists

Oshri Hakak

Oshri is a Los Angeles-based artist and musician. He is a children's book author and illustrator, creating books that touch on mental health, mindfulness, inter-being, and consciousness for ages 2-202. Oshri loves to generate creativity that aids people and communities in our individual and collective healing journeys. He studied psychology and management at Duke University, and is also certified in mediation and dialogue facilitation, as well as yoga instruction.

More of his art can be found on Instagram: @oshrihakak , and his books can be found on www.ButterflyonBooks.com.

Phyllis Karmas

Hi my name is Phyllis. I live in Jupiter, Florida. I am a loving, sweet and creative person. Since I was a child, I was fascinated by color and used drawing to communicate my emotions and feelings. I was speech delayed and cognitively different. I used art as my healing and escape.

Art helped me express my creativity through my emotions at a spiritual level. My purpose is to touch people's hearts through my art and to help them connect with their feelings and emotions at a deeper level. I believe, as a healer myself, in the gift of giving back to humanity through our gifts and talents. I am grateful to have art as my spiritual energy to guide me through my creations.

More Books by Butterflyon Books
www.ButterflyonBooks.com

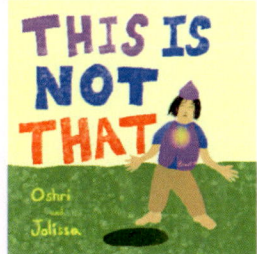

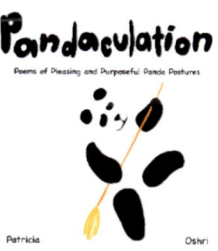

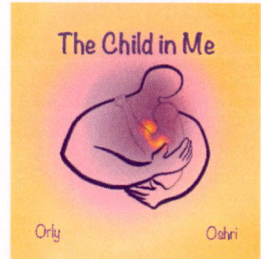

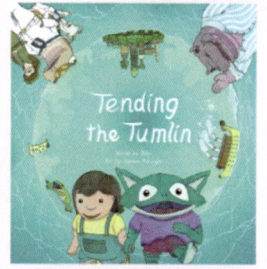

Locker Room Talk
Of Mice, Men and a Bunch of Other Creatures

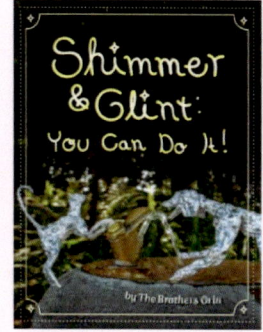

Happy Minutes
a book about making the best of our minutes

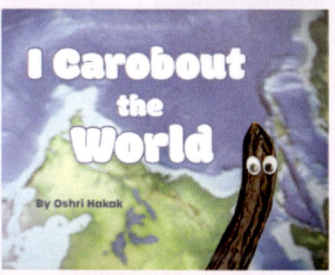

Draw-Wings

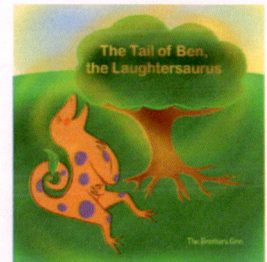

BUTTERFLYON BOOKS